D0929413

To my mom and dad,
Ken and Mary Petzinger,
along with the rest
of my family, for their
unwavering support.

www.mascotbooks.com

BOB THE BANANA GOES BAD

For more information, please contact:
Mascot Books
620 Herndon Parkway, Suite 320
Herndon, VA 20170
info@mascotbooks.com

Library of Congress Control Number: 2020917803

CPSIA Code: PRT1120A
ISBN-13: 978-1-64543-751-2

Printed in the United States

BOB THE BANANA GOES BAD

Steve Petzinger and
Selai Akbar-Hussain
Illustrated by Juan Diaz

One day inside Mr. Abbott's refrigerator, the groceries were having their morning meeting.

Bernie the bagel stood in front of everybody and said, "I, mayor of this refrigerator, want everybody to know that you will all be picked one day. Stay positive, stay fresh!"

A little while later, there was a lot of chatter around the fridge.

"Oh, no! This is terrible!" exclaimed Arvid the apple.

"What is it?" asked Patrick the potato.

"It's Bob the banana—he's gone bad!" Arvid wailed. He pointed toward Bob, the browning banana.

"We'd better tell Bernie the big bagel," Marvin the mustard added.

So, Arvid went to tell Bernie the big bagel.

"What's wrong?" replied Bernie.

Arvid cried, "Bob the banana's gone bad!
I'm sad right down to my core."

"Yes—just thinking about it makes me jiggle,"
added Jerry the jello.

"It makes me shiver," said Ivan the ice cube.

"Well, I've got to do something about this," said Bernie the big bagel. "I am the mayor of this refrigerator, after all."

All of a sudden, Bob the banana busted out of his drawer.

"Here comes Bob the banana!" said April the apricot

“I’m never going to be eaten!”
yelled Bob the banana. “I’ve gone bad!”

"It's okay," said Courtney the corn.

"One day you'll get eaten," said April the apricot.

"You can always become...umm,"
said Courtney the corn.

Then, April the apricot said,
"I know! You can become
banana bread!
Or banana fritters!
Or banana pudding! Yum!"

"Thanks, you guys, for all your support, but it's never going to happen," said Bob the banana. Then, Bob the banana walked away sadly and disappeared.

A little while later...

Betty the blueberry said,
"Bob the banana is gone!"

"We will have to search the refrigerator
for him," said Bernie the big bagel.

The group looked high and low, but Bob the bad banana was nowhere to be found.

"He's not here!" said Arvid the apple.

"He's not over here, either," said Tom the tomato.

"I don't see him!" said Betty the blueberry.

"We seem to be in a pickle," said Pamela the pickle.

Suddenly, Bob the banana appeared. But this time, he was different. He wasn't happy, and he wasn't sad. He was mad.

Bernie the big bagel asked, "Why do you have that look on your face? You look mad."

Bob the banana said, "I've been waiting all day to be picked. You said I would get picked. Courtney and April said I would get picked. But...I'm still here."

Then, Bernie the big bagel replied with a serious look on his face, “Never give up hope.”

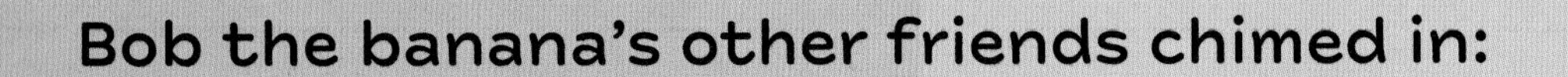

Bob the banana's other friends chimed in:

"One day I'll be squashed!" said Sammy the squash.

"One day I'll be mashed!" said Patrick the potato.

"One day I'll be crushed!" said Tom the tomato.

No matter what anybody said, Bob didn't believe them. It seemed like Bob the banana had given up hope.

Just then, the refrigerator door opened.

There stood Mr. Abbott himself. He seemed hungry.

He picked up
Bob the banana.
Everyone was so
surprised and
happy!

Then, Mr. Abbott said,
"This banana is rotten."

Everyone gasped.

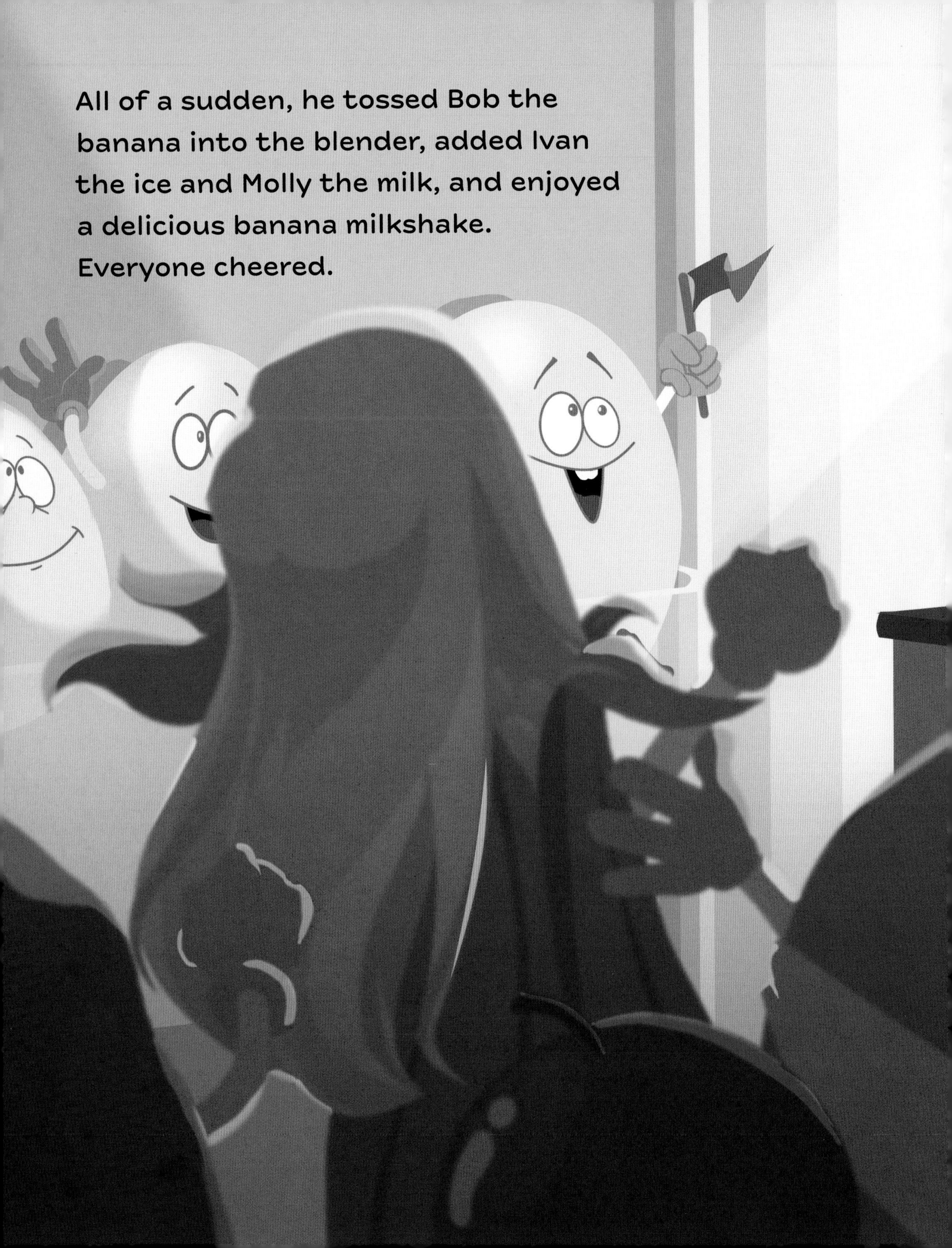

All of a sudden, he tossed Bob the banana into the blender, added Ivan the ice and Molly the milk, and enjoyed a delicious banana milkshake. Everyone cheered.

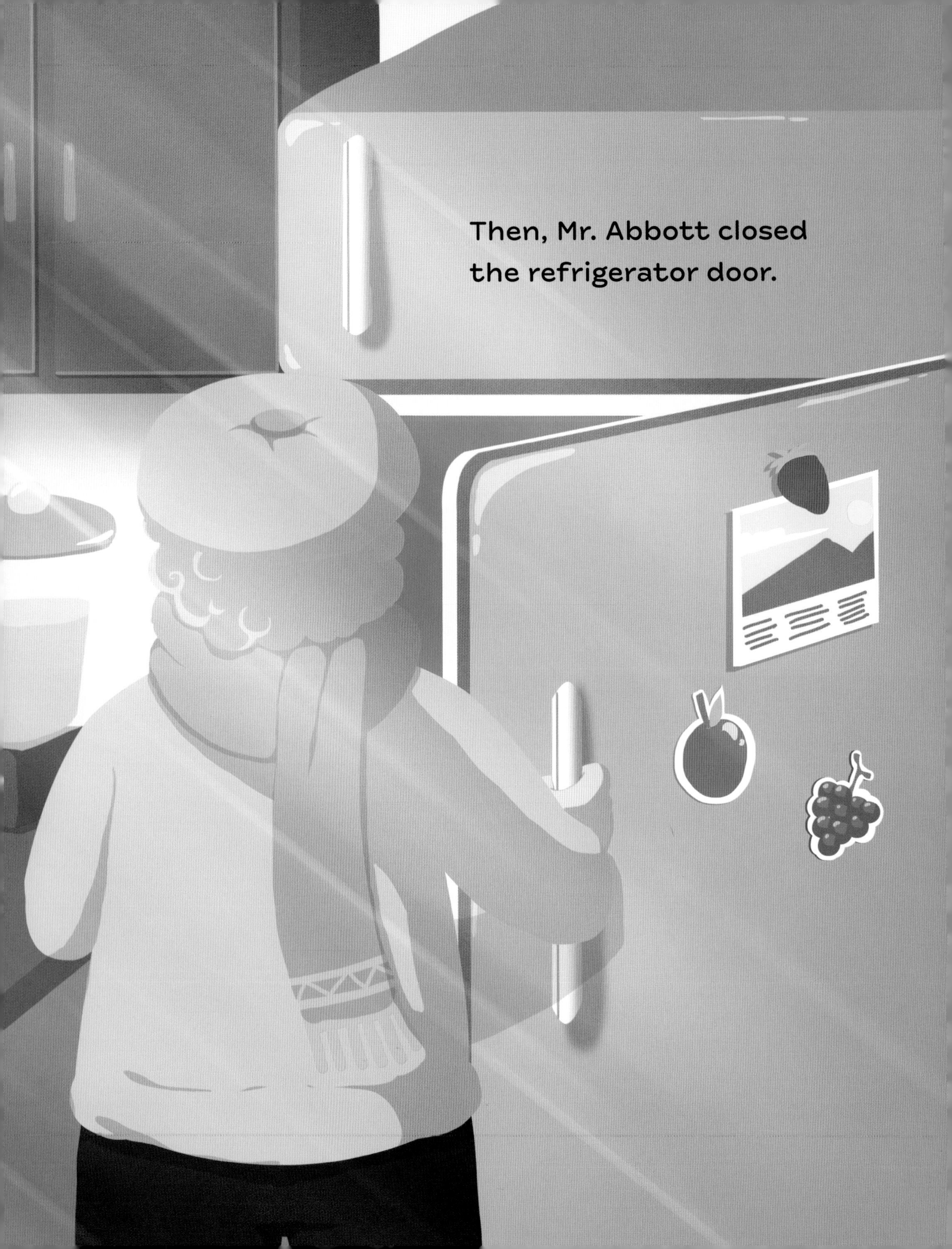

Then, Mr. Abbott closed the refrigerator door.

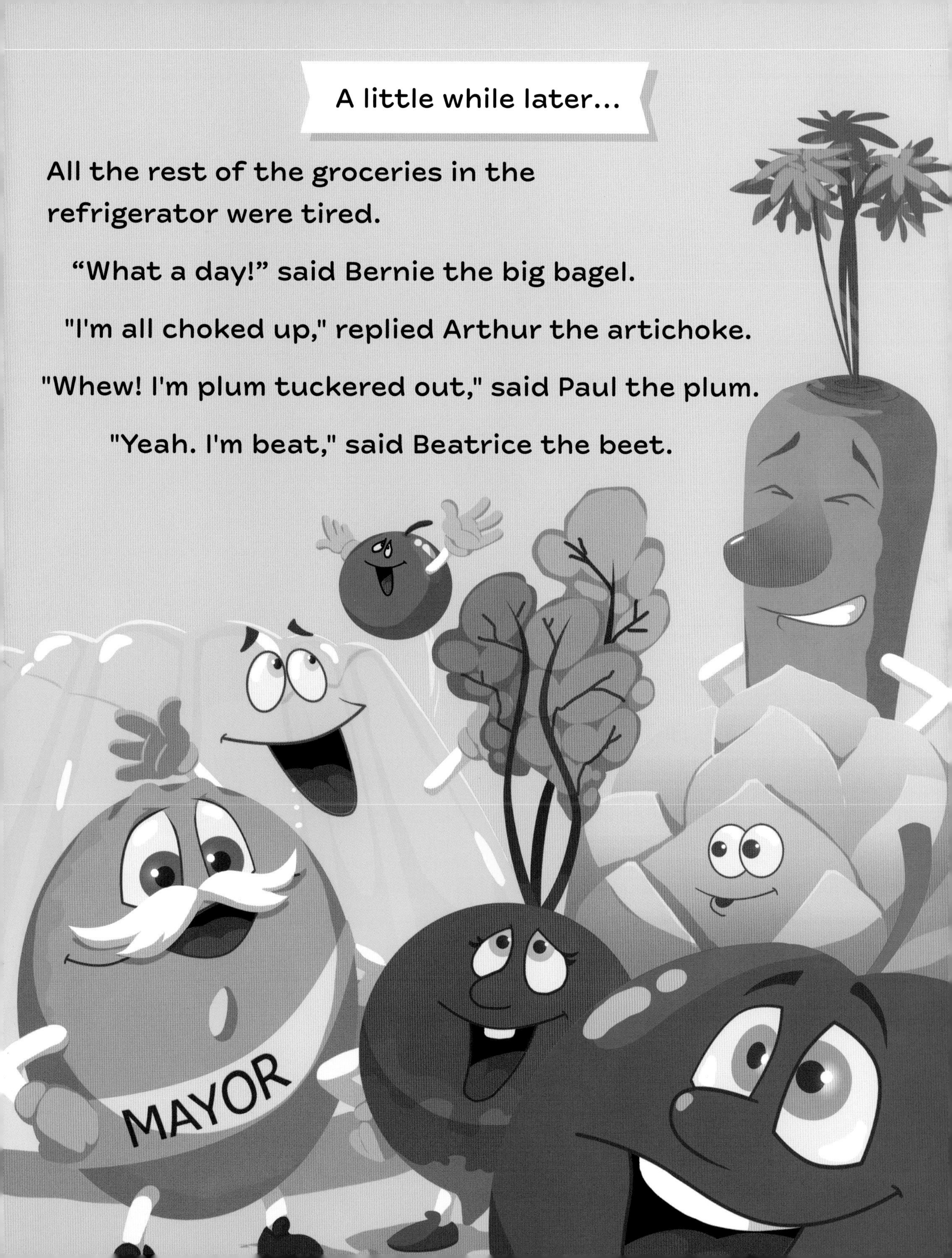
A little while later...
All the rest of the groceries in the refrigerator were tired.
“What a day!” said Bernie the big bagel.
"I'm all choked up," replied Arthur the artichoke.
"Whew! I'm plum tuckered out," said Paul the plum.
"Yeah. I'm beat," said Beatrice the beet.
MAYOR

Now that Bob the banana was finally eaten, everybody could go to sleep.

It turns out Bob wasn't so bad after all!

The End
MAYOR

ABOUT THE AUTHOR

Steve Petzinger first created the concept for *Bob the Banana* when he was just twelve years old. His mother kept the original version, and over the years, his family urged him to publish it. In 2020, he decided to finally take their advice.

ABOUT THE CO-AUTHOR

Steve sought help and expertise from his close friend, Selai Akbar-Hussain, who has been teaching preschool for eight years. She has read hundreds of children's books and is knowledgeable about children's books content. After months of hard work, both their dreams of publishing a children's book came true.